5 Secrets to Effective Communication

To Angela & Wendi,
I miss both of you so much!
I truly hope you will enjoy
this book. I look forward
to your emails.
Keep well!!
Fondly,
Sandy

5 Secrets to Effective Communication

Creating Meaningful
Relationships and Enhanced
Happiness in Your Business Life

SANDY CHERNOFF

SOFT SKILLS FOR SUCCESS

PROMONTORY
P R E S S

Sandy Chernoff, R.D.H., B.Sc.
Soft Skills for Success
www.softskillsforsuccess.com

Editing and proofreading: Marial Shea
Pattern illustration: copyright © Volodymyr Grinko / Thinkstock
Book design, layout and typesetting: Jan Westendorp, Kato Design & Photo

Library and Archives Canada Cataloguing in Publication

Cataloguing data available from Library and Archives Canada

ISBN 978-0-9936562-0-0 (trade paperback)
978-0-9936562-1-7 (epub)
978-0-9936562-2-4 (pdf)
978-0-9936562-3-1 (mobi)

Printed in Canada, by Friesens

Distributed by Promontory Press
www.promontorypress.com

14 15 16 17 18   5 4 3 2 1

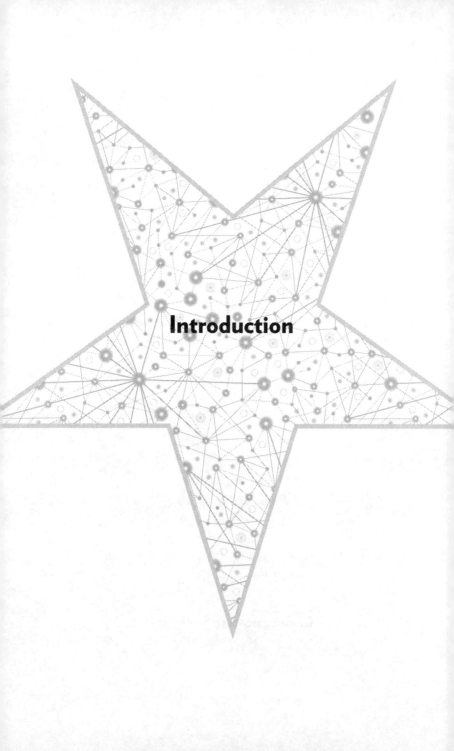

Introduction

THE TOPIC OF COMMUNICATION is a hot one in the business world, and there's a good reason for this. Human beings require direct contact with other humans in order to thrive. Without clear, effective communication how can we establish that necessary contact, build on it, and maintain it so that we can be happy and work productively together?

Today's businesses are moving more and more into collaborative approaches that require effective teamwork to accomplish goals. High-performance teams gain their status through communication that is respectful, trusting, supportive, encouraging, and clear. Whether you are a leader, manager, or member of your team, good communication is what will allow you to achieve your goals while saving you from mistakes, missed deadlines, resentment, and general unhappiness.

Sounds reasonable, right? But what exactly is effective communication? Well, that's what this book is about. Let's start now with my nutshell definition:

> Effective communication means sending messages that are understood by those with whom you are communicating and understanding the messages sent to you.

Many of us believe we are good communicators because we have been doing it since we were born. However, in truth, we don't always understand all the complexities involved in getting across our requests, desires, and ideas. While many of our business transactions are now done online and through our various time-saving devices, we still base them on the trust we build through good communication. This book explores the meaning and practice of effective communication, including:

★ Why Active Listening is the key communication skill, and how to practice it

★ How to become accountable through clear, direct conversations

★ Learning to communicate assertively, and how it's different from being aggressive

★ Adjusting your message for gender differences

★ Tuning communication for different personality types

In addition, I have included a few exercises so you can practice these strategies in the context of your own work and life.

But before we get started, you might be wondering what qualifies me to call myself a communication expert. This book is the result of an interesting and circuitous journey that began almost five decades ago.

For over forty years, I practised clinical dental hygiene in Oregon, California, Ontario, and British Columbia. Along the way I also earned a degree in education, which qualified me to teach clinical and academic courses to members of the dental profession for over thirty years.

During my decades of practice I learned the secret that would form the foundation of my communication strategies: Establishing trusting relationships with my patients resulted in more successful outcomes, both for them and for me.

I discovered that patients who better understood their dental condition, including what would happen if they didn't follow my homecare instructions, were more likely to comply with treatment protocols. In other words, my most important role as a competent dental hygienist was not to just clean their teeth, but to be an impactful educator.

I converted patients into good brushers and flossers because I listened well enough to learn what truly mattered to them. Once I understood them, I could tailor my message to be personally meaningful, inspiring them to change their dental-care behaviour, improve their dental health, and make informed decisions.

Every dental office is a natural team, and I learned how to become a valuable team player, helping create a positive atmosphere and provide the highest level of professional services. What I learned then—and have confirmed during my years as an educator—is that the key element for any high-performance team is clear, honest communication.

In 1996, I was invited by a large international women's organization to become a leadership/motivational trainer. For the next fifteen years, I flew across the continent, from Victoria to New York City, providing seminars to empower women to take on higher roles and responsibilities in their communities. My work always started with the same key step: listening to each group's issues to understand what they needed. Most of the centres I visited were so delighted with the results that they invited me back for more workshops.

With encouragement from my son, Marc, I realized I could marry the people-managing and team-player expertise I had gained as a dental hygienist to my education degree and leadership/motivational training. A perfect combination for building a successful soft skills consulting business!

I started by making cold calls to large law firms. Many of them engaged me to provide staff training, mostly in communication skills, but also in stress management, time management, and organizational skills. I eventually expanded my role as a public speaker, and my business continued to grow.

I love my work. In fact, my credo is, "When I quit having fun, I am done!" I go to work, have loads of fun, meet great people, and get paid. It truly does not get any better!

Why write about communication *at work?* My own team and organizational experience is only part of what inspires me. Another reason I'm passionate about communication in the workplace is because we spend more time at work than with our friends and family. If we do not like our job, it's possible we also do not like our lives. That is truly sad.

I trust you will find that by improving your communication skills you will be able to achieve more of what you desire and at the same time experience more happiness in all that you do! The world still conducts business based on trusted relationships and those are built, maintained, and nourished through Active Listening and clear, honest, and open communication.

So let's get started on this most important topic so you can enjoy a more successful, productive, and creative life.

Secret #1

Active Listening

Opens the Door to

Effective Communication

HEARING IS AN ABILITY,
LISTENING IS AN ART

ACTIVE LISTENING is not only the most important communication skill in the workplace, it is the basis of all effective relationships. An art, a skill, and a discipline, Active Listening is *not* the same as hearing. Merely hearing is what we might call *Passive Listening*, which can put distance between you and the person you're speaking with. With Active Listening, you listen and respond in ways that bring you and the other person closer.

Why is Active Listening important? Well, when we are listened to with respect (that is, when we receive confirming feedback from the listener), we feel like we are being taken seriously and what we have to say matters. Generous listening enhances our well-being, spelling the difference between feeling like a valued part of the team and feeling isolated.

Active Listening broadens us, lays the groundwork for effective collaboration, elevates the quality of our relationships, and empowers team leaders and members to do their best work. Most people will not really listen or pay attention to another person's point of view until they feel they have been heard and understood. If nothing else, Active Listening can make you the most popular person in the room!

Let's look at an example of what can happen when we don't use Active Listening. Have you ever given instructions to a co-worker, asking them to perform a task or run an errand, only to find they did not do what you expected? Well, the fault could be at least partly yours. Just because you told them something doesn't mean they "heard" what you think you said. When you made your request, did you check to see if you had their full attention? Did you ask for feedback from them, and really listen to make sure they received the same message you sent and understood what you wanted them to do?

> Active Listening uses more than just your ears.

When we communicate without checking to see how our message is received—in other words, without Active Listening—we can end up disappointed, frustrated, angry, and resentful. I used to experience this when I began practicing dental hygiene. I would spend twenty minutes giving my patient instructions for brushing and flossing their teeth, pointing out the plaque and bleeding associated with the places they were missing. I would then expect them to go home and practice healthy dental care—after all, I told them and showed them!

When the patient would return six months later with the same spots being missed, and the same amount of bleeding and infection, they might even tell me, "no one has ever showed me this before!" Really! What did that tell me?

I had missed the essential step of listening to find out who they are and what matters to them. Once I'd listened, I would know which "buttons" to press to encourage them to make the changes I was suggesting. By asking for feedback, I would also know what they had heard and understood. And when patients realized that I was listening carefully, they gave me their trust and respect, based on their perception that I sincerely cared about them. All this thanks to Active Listening!

As I learned to listen to my patients, I also shifted my language to use layman's terms rather than "dentalese" when explaining dental procedures, so patients could understand me. For example, if I spoke to them about a carious lesion on the distal of tooth #46, they would likely not have a clue what I was talking about. Much better to point out visible decay at the back end of a molar, identify the tartar and plaque below the gums, or press lightly on their gums to show them how an area of infection was causing pain. The patient was more likely to comply with my directions if I clearly communicated the problem in language they could understand.

ACTIVE LISTENING USES MORE THAN JUST YOUR EARS

You need to use your ears to initially hear a message, along with the tone and volume of the voice. But you also need to "listen" with:

* ★ Your eyes—to observe the non-verbal messages of facial expression, body language, and posture

* ★ Your heart—to perceive the emotional overtones of the delivery

* ★ Your mind—to process what you have perceived and decide what action to take, if any, to achieve the desired outcome

* ★ Your inner perception—to listen within and sense your own reactions

* ★ Your will—because being willing to listen is as important as being able

* ★ Your voice—to ask for feedback and clarify the message

This last point is a crucial part of Active Listening. As a speaker, if you do not receive some concrete feedback you will have NO idea if the other person heard what you think you said, how they computed the information, or what they intend to do with it. And as a listener, you will have no idea if you have understood the other person without checking in with them after they finish speaking. Active Listening will ensure that when you part ways, the two of you are "on the same page."

In my early days of practice as a dental hygienist, I sometimes felt disappointed, frustrated, and resentful due to miscommunication with patients. Once I learned to use Active Listening techniques, I became not only much happier in my work, but also more effective in helping patients change their behaviour.

WHAT ACTIVE LISTENING IS *NOT*

Can an ordinary conversation involve Active Listening? Yes, it can, but Active Listening is much more than just a conversation. We've all had conversations with people who never really listen. Merely being quiet long enough for the other person to talk is not the same as Active Listening!

Listening is *not* solving problems for others. Most especially, it is *not* interrupting people to explain to them what *you* think they should feel, think or do. Often, the experience of being truly heard helps people understand their own problems better and find solutions for themselves. This is why Active Listening is *not* just offering sympathy, as sympathy can interrupt this vital process of self-understanding.

As effective Active Listeners, we put aside our own concerns for the duration of the conversation and listen in a concentrated manner to the concerns of the other person. We listen with empathy and non-judgment to that person's feelings and anxieties, allowing them to express their (possibly ambivalent) feelings to the point where they feel understood.

OBSTACLES TO ACTIVE LISTENING

If Active Listening is such a good idea, what prevents us from using it more often? Let's look at two groups of factors that can work against Active Listening: Interferences and Roadblocks.

Interferences are factors we need to keep in mind when we are the speaker and someone else is listening. They include things our listener is thinking, doing and assuming that we, as the speaker, should try to be aware of.

Roadblocks are factors we need to watch for when we are the listener and someone else is speaking. They include things we might be doing to interrupt and frustrate the speaker. Again, we want to increase our awareness of these factors so we can become better listeners.

> Merely being quiet long enough for the other person to talk is not the same as Active Listening!

For clear communication, we need to make sure the message sent is the one received. Understanding Interferences and Roadblocks helps us do this by increasing our awareness of the listener (when we are speaking) and getting clarification from the speaker (when we are listening). Let's have a look now at six Interferences and seven Roadblocks that can get in our way.

INTERFERENCES: SPEAKER BEWARE!

Interference #1: Your listener is not focusing on the message

Here are two factors that can distract your listener from your message.

★ The average human can mentally process approximately 400 to 800 spoken words per minute, yet the average speaker uses only 125 to 175 words per minute. This can make it difficult for a listener to stay focused.

★ Listeners bring their past with them into the conversation, possibly causing them to be distracted by feelings, values, and attitudes. You as the speaker may say something that triggers a negative memory and evokes an emotional reaction.

Both of these potential distractions can make it difficult for a listener to stay with what we're saying, as they might start to think about their own concerns and miss the message we're sending. Make sure you "listen" to their body language, posture and facial expression so you will know if their attention is wandering or they are experiencing negative emotions. Check in with them by asking them questions like, "Does that make sense to you?" or "Do you have any thoughts on this matter?"

> Interferences are factors we need to keep in mind when we are the speaker and someone else is listening.

Interference #2: Your listener is listening passively

Being passive is much easier than concentrating on your message, but, unfortunately, it leads to ineffective listening. It is difficult to tell whether or not a person is actively engaged in the exchange if they give no definite indication of their interest and focus.

As with Interference #1, observe your listener's body language and try to read how they're responding to your message. Give them more openings to participate in the conversation. Pause more frequently to check in verbally, asking for their feedback and opinions.

Interference #3: Your listener is distracted by the setting

Just as thoughts and feelings can invade your listener's internal perceptual field, outside distractions can invade their external field, distracting them from your message. So, if you are going to have a meaningful exchange, be sure to choose a setting with few or no distractions such as traffic noise, construction, side conversations, business machines, people coming in and out, etc.

This is also true when speaking to a group of people. Audience engagement is key to having an impact on your listeners, so keep external distractions to a minimum.

Interference #4: Your listener is physically uncomfortable

Perhaps your listener is too hot, too cold, tired, not feeling well, or even mulling a problem of their own. Those issues could interfere with their ability to concentrate on your message. Physical needs tend to win out over intellectual needs, so adjust what you can in the environment, observe your listener and check in with them to make sure they have what they need to feel comfortable.

Interference #5: Your listener is confused by unfamiliar language

If you use words and concepts your listener doesn't understand (like when I used complicated "dentalese" as a new hygienist), they may stop listening. They simply might not be willing to expend the extra energy required to understand you, so be sure to match your words with both the cognitive level and language skills of your listener. This can also be true when giving a presentation to an audience. In both one-on-one conversations and speaking to groups, it's up to you to present your ideas using appropriate vocabulary.

Interference #6: Your listener's preconceived ideas are getting in their way

Your listener might not give you a fair hearing because they have preconceived conclusions about you or your topics. They might even put up a mental "wall" that prevents your message from being received. This can also be an obstacle in group presentations.

To guard against this, tune in to your listener or audience. Ask questions to find out what they think about your topic ("Bob, how does this line up with your department's usual process?"). Check in to make sure they don't feel you are speaking either below or above their level of knowledge, otherwise you run the risk of losing them.

ROADBLOCKS: LISTENER BEWARE!

Have you ever tried to talk over a painful problem with a co-worker or friend, only to have them interrupt you with irrelevant advice or a story about their own "similar" experience? You just wanted them to listen to you, and instead they talked about themselves and told you how to "fix" your problem without even really hearing you.

The truth is, when somebody talks to us, our job is to listen, so we need to BE QUIET! When a person is looking for a sounding board, our job is to listen attentively, encouraging them to tell us more. Only when they are done should we offer some solid feedback, validating all they have tried, and suggesting solutions they may not have explored.

The Roadblocks below are some of the key ways we can hijack another person's message. They can disrupt the speaker's train of thought, cause them to forget what they wanted to share, and even suggest that we don't respect them. Putting up these Roadblocks when people speak with us can also deter them from turning to us again in the future.

> When somebody talks to us, our job is to listen, so we need to BE QUIET!

Roadblock #1: Giving unsolicited advice

"You should talk to your boss about it."

When you give another person advice they haven't asked for, you might give them the impression you think they are not as smart as you. Why not wait until you find out if they've already spoken to their boss?

Roadblock #2: Giving advice disguised as questions

"Have you seen a marriage counsellor?"

Asking a leading question like this is really just a polite way of giving advice. Again, they may have done it already and by jumping in with this question you are assuming they have not considered this option. Listen first, ask questions later!

Roadblock #3: Offering superficial reassurance

"Don't worry, you'll feel better about it tomorrow."

This kind of pat reassurance can feel patronizing. It suggests that the speaker's perception of the problem is not valid and that you know better. If they have been experiencing this situation for a while they know they're not likely to feel better tomorrow, so your words are empty.

Roadblock #4: Criticizing

"If you're going to sit around all day staring into space, of course you won't get anything done."

Nobody wants to talk openly with someone who is criticizing them. Unfortunately, we often save this sort of comment for those we love the most. Criticism is not an effective motivating force, and it may make the person less likely to come to you with future issues. To keep the lines of communication open, bite your tongue when you feel the need to criticize!

Roadblock #5: Interrupting

"Say, Mary, that is a truly lovely necklace you are wearing. I would love to get a similar one. Where did you get it?"

You have cut off the person's story with your own unrelated personal thought. This interrupts their train of thought and implies that what you have to say is more important. They may not want to continue speaking with you, or they may avoid coming to you in the future.

If you are inclined to interrupting, you might want to practice listening to *yourself*, to figure out what causes you to do this. Is their story stirring up a painful memory or triggering a negative emotion in you? Are you too tired to focus right now on what they're trying to tell you?

Make it a discipline to wait until the other person gives you a signal that they are finished telling their story before you jump in with feedback or stories of your own.

Roadblock #6: Telling your own stories

"I had the same experience last year." Or: "I know someone who had cancer, and she beat it."

When you make comments like this, you are turning the spotlight onto yourself, making the conversation about you. Keep the focus on them until they pause. THEN you can ask questions or add comments.

Roadblock #7: Not maintaining eye contact

When you look around the room or out the window, the person speaking might feel disrespected, assuming that you are not listening. You might even appear to be searching for someone else to speak with.

Keep your eyes on the other person without staring, to let them know you are paying attention. You can float your eyes across their face to show them that you are listening.

*   *   *

If we increase our awareness of Interferences for our listeners when we are speaking, we can ensure that the message we are sending is received loud and clear. And if we increase our awareness of Roadblocks for speakers when we are listening, we ensure that they feel free to send their message to us in its entirety. Clarity rarely occurs without some feedback, so do not be afraid to ask for it.

WHAT DOES ACTIVE LISTENING LOOK LIKE?

We can take a vital clue from nature as to what Active Listening looks like: We have two ears and one mouth, which points out very clearly that we should be listening twice as much as talking! We cannot learn anything when we are speaking, so if you want to become smarter, listen more.

Let's review. To foster effective communication at work, you need to be a good listener—and that means using Active Listening. Here's what Active Listening involves:

1. First: stop talking! No one can listen and talk at the same time.

2. Develop and demonstrate a keen interest in the other person's opinion or perspective. Keep an open mind and stay visibly engaged during the exchange.

3. Stay focused on what the other person is saying so as not to miss any important points. To do this, you need to be able to block out inner and outer distractions.

4. Refrain from interrupting until the speaker finishes what they wish to say. Make mental notes of what you might wish to add or questions you may have, so you can bring them up at the end. You do not want to be rude or disruptive to the speaker's train of thought.

5. Be aware of body language. When you're listening, nod, smile (when appropriate), maintain eye contact, be encouraging and attentive. Do *NOT* shuffle papers, look around, check your cell phone, or fidget. And when you're speaking, notice what

your listener's body language is telling you about how they're receiving your message.

6. Be patient, some people take time to explain their issue or concern. Again, keep an open mind, as prejudice can show in your body language and remarks. Concentrate on the facts in a non-judgmental fashion and put the other person at ease. Try *NOT* to disagree, argue, or criticize. Just listen!

7. Ask questions to make sure you have understood what the speaker has said. You can even paraphrase some of what you heard. This is good feedback for the speaker, as it shows you did truly listen respectfully to what they had to say.

8. Again, *stop talking!* You cannot listen and talk at the same time.

Learning to practice Active Listening should lead to less conflict and miscommunication, and greater productivity, creativity, and happiness at work, and in all aspects of your life!

ACTIVE LISTENING EXERCISE

Review the Interferences and Roadblocks and ask yourself if there are any areas you could strengthen, either
when you are speaking or lis-
tening. Think about difficult
conversations you have had
with colleagues or clients over
the years. Are there particular
Interferences or Roadblocks
that tend to trip you up?

> We cannot learn anything
> when we are speaking, so if
> you want to become smarter,
> listen more.

Jot down the points that are most relevant to you
and review them regularly, especially before a potentially contentious meeting or conversation. Be creative
with using language that works for you. For example,
if you respond well to affirmations, you might want to
replace "Don't interrupt" with something like "I enjoy
giving other people the space to freely tell their stories."

KEY TAKEAWAY POINTS FROM
SECRET #1: ACTIVE LISTENING

1. Hearing is an ability; listening is an art: use your ears, your eyes, your heart, your will and your mind if you wish to be an Active Listener.

2. If you are going to hear and learn anything, you need to stop talking!

3. Focus on the speaker, encourage them with non-verbals, maintain eye contact, and provide feedback to let them know that you have received the message they sent.

4. When you are the speaker, be aware of the Interferences that prevent your listener from focusing on and understanding your message, and develop strategies to overcome them.

5. When you are the listener, avoid the Roadblocks. Showing your speaker respect will encourage them to communicate openly and honestly.

Secret #2

Accountability

Leads to Personal

Empowerment

TAKING BACK CONTROL

WHEN SOMEONE TREATS us in a negative or hurtful way, we can feel powerless, frustrated, angry, and resentful. We might focus on blame and make excuses as to why we find ourselves in this situation. We might think, "why does this always happen to me?!"

Being accountable means taking responsibility for our inner reactions, and for what we say and do. It means taking control of situations and solving problems instead of blaming others and making excuses. One of the most powerful ways of taking control is through clear, direct communication.

When we get stuck in blame, our sense of reality gets skewed, and this affects our ability to communicate in a meaningful, appropriate manner. We all know people who live their lives in "victim mode." They are difficult to endure for very long as they tire us out, depress us, and drag us down.

> When we take charge of difficult situations and communicate our feelings and needs clearly, we feel empowered.

Fortunately, the opposite is also true: When we take charge of difficult situations and communicate our feelings and needs clearly, we feel empowered. We are also affected positively by being around those who can and do take charge, especially when there are issues that make others uncomfortable.

THE ACCOUNTABILITY TRUTH

While it is only human to feel like a victim when something negative happens to us, we always have choices.

I developed what I call the Accountability Truth as a guide for when we're faced with choosing between being a "victim" and a "victor."

> The Accountability Truth = I contribute to the
> problems I experience.

I suggest you adapt this to your own beliefs. As an example, here's my personal Accountability Truth, and the one I teach clients:

> When you and I, or any two people interact,
> each is 50% responsible for what we co-create.

I coach people to take 100% responsibility for their 50%!

Let's look at accountability in action. A client I'll call Lea shared this story during a workshop I presented.

When Lea landed her first job as a legal secretary, the lawyer who hired her already had two secretaries who had been working there for several years. The lawyer was a very busy single practitioner. Every morning she met with her staff and berated them for various issues and then gave them instructions for the day.

Being berated made them all start the day feeling bad, which of course negatively affected their performance.

Lea would talk with her parents about this after work, sometimes even breaking into tears. Lea's dad noticed that this situation was really bothering her. After many months, he took her aside and suggested that she either speak to her boss or leave the position, as it was obviously taking a toll on her.

The next morning, Lea reluctantly spoke to her co-workers about her dad's advice. They were afraid to join in on this difficult conversation but agreed to be there when she spoke with their boss. Following the boss's usual "tirade," Lea asked her if she was unhappy with the quality of work the staff was delivering. The lawyer answered, "of course not, or I would not keep you here!"

Lea continued, "Then why do you reprimand us each morning? It lowers our self-esteem and impacts negatively on our ability to perform at our best. If you have specific issues, we'd appreciate it if you would let us know. Otherwise, we feel it would greatly enhance our productivity to begin our day on a more positive note."

The lawyer ran out of the room in tears! Shocked by this response from her confident boss, Lea figured she would be out of a job. However, at the end of the day, the lawyer called Lea into her office and said, "Thank you so much for letting me know the effect I was having on all of you. I had no idea I was upsetting you. In the future that will no longer be happening. I truly value the contributions you make and I know I could not produce this volume of work without your support and efficiency."

For many years, the four of them worked together well. In fact, all was peaceful until the practice grew and the lawyer hired more staff. Her tirades returned—but only for the new staff. Looks like they will have to learn to be accountable too!

THE ACCOUNTABILITY OPTIONS

When we feel victimized by someone's actions or communication, we have three basic options. Each of them requires that you communicate honestly—at least with yourself, and possibly with others too:

1. **Take action:** Ask yourself if there's a way to change the situation. If you think there is, then take positive action. This could involve being assertive and having a difficult conversation with whoever made you feel like a victim. It might even be as simple as stating what you need to the appropriate person.

2. **Manage your attitude:** Have an honest conversation with yourself about the situation. Face what's really going on and what your role might be, if any. See if you can change your perception of the situation so you can be at peace with it and stop talking and thinking about it. Develop an appropriate strategy for dealing with the issue.

3. **Leave the situation:** If things cannot be fixed, save yourself and leave.

Once you decide to deal with a bad situation in one of these three ways, you can move on with your life. Dealing with problems rather than letting them fester offers us a much better chance for clear, open, and honest communication.

Let's take a closer look at each of these three options.

Take action

Taking action will always make us feel better because it gives us a sense of taking back control. In taking action, we focus on a useful approach and move toward a new result. This feels much better than complaining and blaming.

If the problem is a leak in your roof, a funny noise in your car, or a sick pet, it's not that hard to figure out what to do and get down to doing it. However, if it relates to an issue with another individual, a more complicated and stressful action might be called for: *having a difficult conversation.*

Most of us hate confrontations and will avoid this option. However, if you don't point out to this person how they have caused you grief, you have no hope of resolving your problem. "If you do not ask, you do not get." Having this conversation does not guarantee your desired outcome, but you will feel better for having tried something positive.

Example of taking action

We all have airport stories. Here is mine.

Several years ago, after attending a training course, a friend dropped me off at the airport for my flight home. Checking in, I discovered that my 7 p.m. flight had been cancelled. The woman in front of me was on the same flight and she was screaming at the agent as if it were the agent's fault that there were no other flights until 11:30 that night.

When it was my turn to check in for the same flight, the agent appeared to ready herself for another onslaught of anger. But I had decided to make myself accountable for my situation, so I told her I understood her position and asked (1) Could she give me a pass for the executive lounge so I could spend the five-hour wait in comfort and quiet? (2) Could I secure a row of seats in the middle section of the plane so I could flip up the arm rests and lie down for this red-eye?

I took action by treating the agent with courtesy instead of blaming her for something beyond *her* control. I also asked for concessions that would make a real difference to me—and that were within her power to give. She was most helpful and granted both my requests.

Remember the Accountability Truth? Here's where that comes in. I asked myself who was to blame for this situation. It certainly wasn't the agent's fault. And it wasn't in any way *my* fault—or was it? I realized that if I had checked the flight status before leaving for the airport, I would not have been stuck waiting there for hours. Blame was not related to the reality of the situation, nor was it a useful option. So I assumed 100 percent responsibility for my own role and took action.

Manage your attitude

If you have tried taking an action (such as having a difficult conversation) and it hasn't resulted in a positive change, it could be time to change something you *can* control: your own attitude. Your goal here is not to change the situation (since you already tried that), but instead to change how you *feel* about it and *react* to it. You want to shift your own perceptions so you can quit thinking and complaining about the situation, and being disappointed or frustrated.

Your choices here are limited only by your imagination. Here are some possibilities:

★ Choose your battles

★ Train yourself to let go of what's aggravating you (for example, ask yourself if it will matter two years from now)

★ Design a "game" you can play in your head so the annoying person's behaviour becomes funny or fun (for example, set a mental timer to see how long it takes before they do their annoying thing)

★ Schedule in flex time to deal with difficult people so you will not be stressed and burdened by their questions, concerns, or whatever makes them difficult

★ Create scenarios in your mind that help deflect the disrespect

Whatever it takes to make the intolerable, tolerable— do it!

Example of managing your attitude

Are you the oldest in your family? Is the youngest a sister or brother and the only one of that gender in your family? Well, in mine, that is the situation. I am the oldest of three and the youngest is the boy. With two older sisters, he essentially grew up with three mothers, who did pretty much everything for him. We taught him to believe that he was the most important person and he did not need to take responsibility for much of anything.

Not surprisingly, this carried on into adulthood. They say you get the behaviour you tolerate, and that's certainly true here. Checking in with the Accountability Truth, I can see that I contributed to my brother's sense of entitlement by perpetuating the coddling.

By a cruel twist of fate, I ended up working for him. Now I needed to try and separate our professional relationship from our familial one—or I might "kill" him at the office one day! So, I decided to take action. I learned how to get his attention by starting a conversation about financial outcomes. From there I would state whatever was bothering me. However, after several of these conversations with no change in outcome, I realized that altering this person's behaviour was unlikely and I had better come up with a Plan B.

On to managing my attitude! I needed a strategy that allowed me to let go of the unimportant issues, choose my battles, and deal with him without having so many "stomach aches." In all fairness, he did not likely realize he made me so crazy!

So here is what I did: I chose my battles and tried to imagine what his perspective would be so I could predict what he would do. If I could correctly predict his behaviour, I would "win." And I got the prize whether I was right or not: the situation became fun instead of annoying and aggravating.

Leave the situation

If you have tried both taking action and managing your attitude and you're still struggling, it may be time to save yourself and walk away. Sometimes, no matter what we do, we are not able to live with a situation. To prevent ourselves from becoming ill, we need to remove ourselves from a job or a relationship that is toxic to us. Only you can save yourself!

If it is to be . . . it is up to me!

Example of leaving the situation

I worked in an office with a difficult boss for a few years. I tried taking action several times to address his rude and unprofessional behaviour in the office. This would work for short periods, if at all.

Next, I tried to come up with a workable strategy to manage my attitude and not let his behavior bother me so much. That really did not work as his challenging behaviour was so frequent.

Finally, as things got even worse, I consulted a labour lawyer and he urged me to quit—immediately. I had been with this practice for a long time and felt loyal to the clients, so this was heartwrenching. But I did do it! I instantly felt relief. Sometimes we just have to save ourselves.

Stuff happens to everybody. Some of it is unfair. Life is unfair. When facing problems, none of the three Accountability Options is easy. Learn to change what you can or manage your attitude. Use clear, open, honest, and respectful conversations whenever possible. And if none of that works, start planning your departure. To have a happy life, you do need to assume 100 percent responsibility for what you *can* change—and take back control!

**Your attitude is the one thing over which you
have total control.
This is being a victor, not a victim.**

ACCOUNTABILITY EXERCISE

Get out your favourite pen and notebook, or your laptop, and describe a situation that has you feeling resentful, disappointed, or confused. Maybe it's something you find yourself complaining about to others. Write down everything that comes to mind. Also jot down how you feel as you write. What emotions are coming up? How do you feel when you're in this situation? Are there ways you feel like a victim?

Now, dig a little deeper and think about the Accountability Truth: What are you contributing to this problem? How can you take 100 percent responsibility for your role, however small? Or if the circumstances are totally out of your control, what can you do to manage your attitude? How would you know if it's time to leave? What practical plans would you have to put in place to get out of the situation? Resolve to apply the Accountability Options to this difficult situation until you no longer have a "stomach ache" regarding this issue.

Remember, the Accountability Options can be hard to do, but being a victor feels so much better in the long run than being a victim. Using clear, open, honest, and respectful communication will bring you more win/win outcomes and much more happiness in your life. Even if you do not get the result you wish, at least you will feel better for taking back control in whatever ways you can.

You cannot make people change their behaviour. However, if you change yours by communicating more clearly, you may be pleasantly surprised by the outcome!

KEY TAKEAWAY POINTS FROM
SECRET #2: ACCOUNTABILITY

1. Take back control by having a difficult conversation when necessary.

2. Manage your perception of the situation. This is another way to take back control. Make this strategy fun if you can. Otherwise, find ways to communicate honestly and respectfully.

3. When all else fails, save yourself and move on. No one can help you if you do not help yourself.

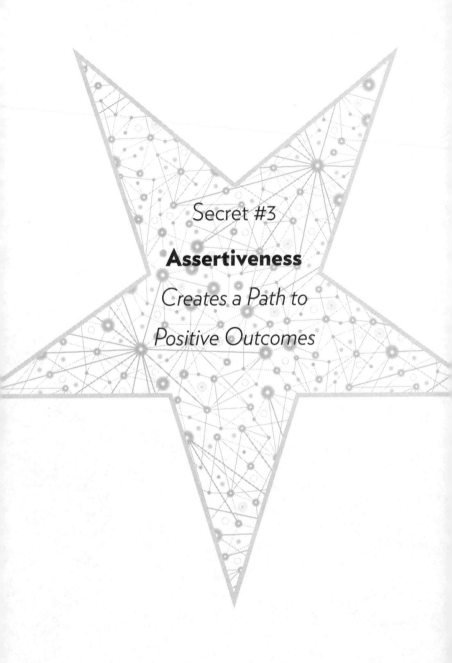

Secret #3

Assertiveness

Creates a Path to

Positive Outcomes

THE ART OF ASKING FOR
WHAT YOU WANT

O NCE YOU DECIDE to be accountable for a difficult situation, being assertive is one of the most effective tools you can use. Assertiveness involves speaking up in an honest and respectful manner, describing your experience, and asking for what you want.

This chapter guides you through preparing for a difficult conversation, recognizing your own patterns and using what I call the "levels of assertiveness." Using these guidelines will help you avoid crossing the line from assertive (honest and respectful) to aggressive (blaming and insulting).

WHY HAVE DIFFICULT CONVERSATIONS?

Many of us will do anything to avoid confrontation. There are times, however, when the best—or even the only—path to resolution is to have a difficult conversation. Only by having that uncomfortable exchange can we at least try to achieve a different outcome when dealing with a troublesome individual.

Those of us who avoid dealing with issues can end up with stress-related illnesses. At the very least, we might find ourselves continually complaining and acting disappointed, frustrated, or resentful, none of which make us a popular companion or co-worker. If we don't speak up, our offender may not realize they have caused us grief and, therefore, will not see a reason to discontinue their problematic or hurtful behaviour. Finally, if we avoid taking assertive action, we run the risk of staying stuck in "victim" mode.

To restate this in the positive, speaking up for yourself assertively has the potential to:

★ Lower your stress, and your chances of developing stress-related illnesses

★ Lessen negativity (both your internal self-talk and external complaining) so you are happier and easier to work with

★ Give your difficult person valuable information that can help them change their actions

★ Help you feel more in control—victor instead of victim

Human beings are creatures of habit who do not readily embrace change. It's good to remember this before initiating a difficult conversation. We cannot make people do things they don't want to do. We can, however, offer them compelling reasons to consider altering their behaviour. People may well surprise us by responding positively. At the very least, they may view us in a new light because our assertiveness was not what they expected. We might earn their respect for attempting to resolve differences in an honest and straightforward manner.

Remember,

"If you do not ask, you do not get."

HOW *NOT* TO BE ASSERTIVE

There is a strategy to conducting a successfully assertive conversation. Before I introduce my strategy, let's review some negative communication styles and self-sabotaging "flip-flop" patterns that *do not* make for positive outcomes in difficult conversations.

WATCH FOR NEGATIVE COMMUNICATION STYLES

Aggressive

An aggressive communication style involves putting people down, blaming others, and/or insulting them. There is a fine line between being aggressive and being assertive. Stay on the assertive side of that line by staying honest and respectful.

Aggressive behavior: strong tone, punishing attitude, you-messages (which can feel like finger pointing and blaming, so are not well received).

Passive

Being passive involves avoiding dealing with the conflict, refusing to undertake a confrontation.

Passive behavior: indirect communication, sounding confused, hinting, procrastinating.

Passive-aggressive

Being passive-aggressive is another way of avoiding conflict. It involves showing anger in indirect ways.

Passive-aggressive behavior: sarcasm, indirect cutting remarks, stubborn resistance, repeated failure to follow directions or complete tasks as requested.

You may have family members, friends, co-workers, or even customers or clients who bring out these negative behaviors in you. How can we practice assertiveness with these people? What behaviors are most likely to help us feel like victors and get us to a win/win outcome?

KNOW YOUR "FLIP-FLOP" PATTERNS

Along with negative communication styles, we can sabotage ourselves by engaging in these three common patterns that interrupt positive focus:

1. **Bad timing:** You **wait too long,** then overreact and "whomp" your gunnysack (filled with all the "next time, I'm really going to tell her . . . "). If you ignore what is bothering you and wait for months before speaking to the person about your concerns, they might not know what you are talking about.

2. **Wrong place:** You **take your anger or frustration out in the wrong place,** often with people you care about most, people who are not the source of the problem. When frustration and anger build up, sometimes you cannot hold them in anymore, and you blow up at the wrong person for a small, inconsequential issue, leaving the real issue unresolved.

3. **No follow-through:** You're a **one-shot strategist** who cannot stand your ground. You say it once, and when your difficult person slips back into the behavior you don't like, you give up and do not point out the problem again. In most cases, having that difficult conversation once will not solve the problem, so be prepared to revisit the issue until the desired results are accomplished.

None of these approaches is effective in gaining a win/win outcome. Focus your efforts at the right time (before your emotions get the best of you), in the right place (with the difficult person, not innocent friends and family), and with follow-through (keep speaking your truth for as long as it's working). Remember, there will always be some people who will NOT give you what you want. In these cases, you may have to resort to changing how you handle the situation for yourself.

Our relationships are like ritual dances: you dip and they dip, you turn and they turn. If you change the dance step, it does not guarantee that the person will change theirs. You may, however, get their attention

and inspire them to view you in a different light, perhaps with more respect—and possibly, just possibly
encourage a change in them.

THE FOUR LEVELS OF ASSERTIVENESS

I employ a structure for assertive conversations that I
call the *Four Levels of Assertiveness:*

Level 1	State your case pleasantly.
Level 2	State it stronger.
Level 3	Promise a consequence.
Level 4	Carry through on the consequence.

This structure can help you know where you are now
with your difficult person or problem, where you want
to go, and how to get the best possible outcome. It can
also help you answer questions like these:

1. What is my goal in having this conversation?

2. Which mode of communication will result in a
   win/win outcome?

3. Do I have the power to suggest consequences for this individual if they don't comply with my request?

4. What will I do to sustain my assertiveness after the conversation?

To illustrate these four levels, here's an example from my days as a dental hygienist. In one dental office I worked in, I shared my operatory with another person. I was rather particular about my work area and at the end of each day, I would thoroughly clean the operatory, refill all the supplies, and set up for future workdays.

When I returned to work on alternate days, I would find the operatory untidy or even dirty, the supplies low, and instruments missing. On several occasions I very respectfully pointed out the deficiencies and explained that I performed these tasks before leaving to allow me more time in the morning to go over my charts for the day and prepare for patients (*Level 1, state your case pleasantly*). She made excuses like "we were busy" and "we ran late," and her behaviour continued.

I suggested that she come in early to deal with the cleanup, telling her I would appreciate her cooperation, since we shared the unit. I also let her know that I would prefer to resolve this between the two of us, but that I would involve the dentist if she didn't respond (*Level 2, state it stronger* and *Level 3, promise a consequence*). She agreed but didn't change her actions.

After speaking to her repeatedly, I finally explained the situation to the dentist and asked for his support (*Level 4, follow through on the consequence*). This was not how I had hoped to solve the conflict, but as she did not respond to my respectful requests (*Levels 1* and **2**), even when I "threatened" to speak to the "boss" about it (*Level 3*), I had to carry out my consequence (*Level 4*). She did comply once the dentist spoke to her, for which I was grateful.

HOLDING A SUCCESSFUL ASSERTIVE CONVERSATION

Don't just walk into a potentially difficult conversation hoping to "wing it." To maximize your success and minimize conflict, it is important that you prepare. Here are four steps that will help you get ready for a difficult conversation:

1. Clarify your purpose

2. Use the Clear Message Format

3. Learn how to say what you want to say

4. Practice the conversation

Clarify your purpose

Ask yourself the following questions to clarify your purpose, troubleshoot possible problems, and define what outcome you're hoping for:

★ What is my purpose for having the conversation?

★ What do I hope to accomplish?

★ What is the ideal outcome?

★ What assumptions am I making about the other person's reaction to the conversation?

★ What "hot buttons" exist—for me and for the other person?

★ How is my attitude toward the conversation contributing to the intended outcome?

Discuss your answers with Human Resources, peers, or other appropriate helpers to be sure you're comfortable with them.

Use the Clear Message Format

The *Clear Message Format* is a structure you can use to successfully navigate through an assertive conversation. It comprises the following three parts (although in practice, they may not be as distinct as they are in theory):

★ **Describe the problematic behaviour or situation objectively,** without judgment words

★ **State what you experience** as a result of that behaviour, including how it makes you feel

★ **Make a polite, specific request**

Getting the results you are seeking depends on using very direct and clear instructions. When using a Clear Message Format keep in mind that you can:

★ Deliver elements in mixed order

★ Work the message to suit your personal style

★ Combine two elements (for example, express your feelings while making a request)

Be sure to put yourself in the other person's shoes during your preparation. This will help you to choose your words and body language appropriately and anticipate their objections. Your openness will invite them to drop their defences and listen. Keep this in mind as you consider how you will open the conversation. Here are some options, which you can tailor for your specific situation:

★ "I'd like to talk to you about _____."

★ "I want to better understand your point of view. Can we talk about _____?"

★ "I'd like to talk about _____. I think we may have different ideas on how to _____."

Learn HOW to say what you want to say

To further strengthen your message, keep in mind that what you say will not produce clear communication if you do not have matching body language. People pay attention much more to how you say it.

For example, think about this sentence: "I did not say you stole my bike." You can change the meaning by emphasizing different words. Emphasize "I" and you suggest someone else said this. Emphasize "say" and you suggest you didn't say it. Emphasize "stole" and you suggest that maybe they borrowed your bike. Emphasize "my" and you suggest it was someone else's bike.

In a difficult conversation, HOW you say what you say has a particularly strong effect—often a much greater effect than the words you are saying. For example, your tone of your voice could be sarcastic, patronizing, sneering, or angry. Your facial expression, body stance, and gestures could be conveying emotions well beyond what's in your words. Some studies suggest that over 90% of your message could be communicated non-verbally when a conversation gets emotional.

Consider that if your non-verbal message does not support and reinforce your words, the listener will not "hear" your verbal message no matter how carefully and appropriately you have crafted it.

Keep the following factors in mind as you speak. They are all ways of controlling *how* you deliver your message:

- ★ **Eye contact:** Do not stare, but float your eyes in a band across the other person's face. This will indicate that you are listening, and you will receive more attention when you are speaking.

- ★ **Body posture:** Face the person squarely, sit up straight or stand appropriately, letting confidence show in your body. Do not cross your arms.

- ★ **Gestures:** Avoid pencil or finger pointing or tapping, hair twirling, money rattling, phone fiddling, knuckle cracking, or any other distracting actions.

- ★ **Voice tone:** As we get excited, our voice usually rises. Keep your voice in the low range. This is especially important for women. Sarcasm and patronizing or disdainful tones will definitely not match respectfully chosen words. Don't end sentences with a question tone if they are statements.

★ **Voice volume:** People won't work to hear you, so keep the volume high enough to be heard. However, you don't want to sound angry, so don't shout.

★ **Language choice:** Try to avoid using confrontational language. For example, when responding, try NOT to use the word "but," as it can negate everything the person just said and inflame the exchange. Instead, use however, nonetheless, so, and, yet, etc.

★ **Facial expression:** Be aware of what you look like when having the exchange. Practice in front of a mirror and get feedback from friends or family before having the conversation. If your expression does not match the words, you will be sending the wrong message and will not end up with the outcome you wish.

★ **Location:** Choose a location that is comfortable and convenient for you, such as your office or a neutral place. You do not want your "opponent" to have the advantage of the location.

★ **Distance:** Pay attention to how close you are to the other person and do not invade their space. (Remember the *Seinfeld* episode where they made fun of the "close talker.")

When you're having the conversation, keep these points in mind:

★ **Pay attention to emotional content** that might be triggered. It is as important as the facts.

★ **Stay focused on your purpose.** Don't be side-tracked.

★ **Stay open.** Maintain an attitude of inquiry and discovery. Set aside assumptions and try to learn as much as possible about the other person's point of view.

★ **Use Active Listening!** Acknowledge that you've heard them by repeating their argument back to them. You don't have to agree. Saying, "it sounds like this issue is very important to you" doesn't mean that you have to change your perspective. Let them complete what they have to say without interruption.

★ **Advocate for your position without diminishing theirs.** State your position concisely and clarify points they may not have understood.

★ **End with problem solving.** Find mutual areas where you can agree on solutions and identify what steps need to be taken. If there is no common ground, return to inquiry.

Practice the conversation

After you clarify your purpose, learn the Clear Message Format and understand *how* to say what you want to say, there's one more crucial step: **practice the conversation.**

If you just want to plan out your Clear Message Format and find the best language for practicing WHAT you want to say, you can rehearse the conversation in your mind. But if you want to get a feel for

HOW to say it, you might want to practice in front of a mirror or with your supervisor, Employee Assistance Program, Human Resources, family, or friend.

By watching yourself or having someone else watch you, you can check for any non-verbal cues you are giving. You can get feedback about how you look and sound before having that difficult conversation. After all, you do not want to drown out your respectful, honest words by covering them up with negative and confrontational non-verbal messages.

NEGATIVE REACTIONS TO ASSERTIVENESS

Even if you are brave enough to entertain an assertive exchange with a difficult person without becoming aggressive, they may not react positively. It is human nature for people to feel "criticized" in these situations. They might become confrontational, using denial and insults. By joining them in their nastiness, you're headed for a lose/lose outcome when what you want is win/win!

Make it difficult for the other person to be unreasonable toward you by staying resolutely honest and polite. If they insist on responding negatively, suggest that you continue the conversation another time.

Here's an example of an aggressive person who tested my ability to stay polite. I was editing an organizational newsletter and she was a contributor who arrived after the deadline with her submission in an unedited format. We routinely sent out notices to contributors regarding layout, format and deadlines, so she had been informed about our requirements. When we told her we could not accept her late and unedited submission, she railed at us that her content was very important and should be accepted regardless of the rules.

I explained very assertively that we had let everyone know far in advance what the requirements for submission were and we expected compliance from all contributors. As she continued to yell about how important her project was, I continued to calmly and respectfully explain that for us to meet our deadline we needed camera-ready copy and we needed it last week. I explained that to handle her materials, we would all have to stay late, which was particularly unfair given that we were all volunteers.

In the end, I acknowledged that her project was important and offered to accommodate some of her copy if she stopped yelling at us, which she did. I managed to maintain my dignity, remaining honest and respectful in the face of her outrage. When she finally left, somewhat placated, the rest of the team applauded. For succeeding editions, she delivered her material on time, and some of it was actually camera-ready!

Following are just two of the negative responses you might get when speaking assertively, and how to counteract them:

The Chill

The person sulks or pouts, often for weeks. It is very uncomfortable and is one of the reasons people do not continue to be assertive.

What to do: *Be assertive about The Chill.*

"Two days ago I spoke to you about_____.
Since then you have not spoken to me in

meetings. This communication pattern is not productive, and I would like us to be able to talk things out."

The Blowup

The person gets angry, and says awful things to you.

What to do: *Be assertive about The Blowup. Remember that they are feeling out of control.*

> "I know you are feeling upset. However, yelling is not productive. Let's discuss this calmly."

DO YOUR BEST AND LET GO OF THE REST!

In the end, even if you do not end up with the ideal, hoped-for outcome, you will feel better for having taken action through a calm, respectful, and honest conversation. Remember, you can always resort to changing your attitude with an appropriate strategy or, if all else fails, walking away to save yourself.

Use unfortunate experiences with difficult people as stepping stones toward a happier future with more win/win outcomes, *not* as roadblocks to your happiness and success! Any mistakes you make are opportunities to learn how to be a more effective communicator.

> To maximize your success and minimize conflict, it's important that you prepare.

ASSERTIVENESS EXERCISE

Bring to mind a person who has disrespected or disappointed you, or caused you to feel resentful—someone you have not yet spoken with. Work through the steps in "Holding a Successful Assertive Conversation." Ask yourself **clarifying questions,** plan out how you can use the **Clear Message Format,** and **practice the conversation.**

Then, if you feel ready, approach your difficult person and ask them to have a conversation with you. Remember, they may feel criticized, so they are unlikely to receive this message happily. Try to keep your tone and facial expressions pleasant, and be respectful and honest in your retorts. Keep coming back to your request and try NOT to use the word "but," as it negates everything the other person has just said, so will not endear you to them.

If they get nasty, just say that you understand and suggest that they think about what you have told them and perhaps you can speak about this again tomorrow after they have had a chance to consider your perception of the situation. Even if you do not get what you want, you will feel better for taking back control.

KEY TAKEAWAY POINTS FROM SECRET #3: ASSERTIVENESS

1. Speaking up assertively is good for your health and your relationships.

2. To get the best possible response in difficult conversations, know and avoid your negative communication styles and flip-flop patterns.

3. Plan your conversation using the Four Levels of Assertiveness.

4. Clarifying your purpose and using the Clear Message Format will help you stay on track during the conversation.

5. Carefully prepare what you are going to say, how it will sound and what you will look like while delivering your message. Be sure to remember that the non-verbal part of your message may outweigh what you say, so be careful not to negate your honest and respectful words with a negative or confrontational tone of voice or body language.

6. Prepare for the reaction of the person with whom you are going to have this conversation. Remember, they are NOT likely to be happy about it.

7. Stay honest and respectful when having a difficult conversation.

8. Know that you may not get what you want; however, you will feel better for trying. You may need to do this more than once.

Secret #4

Adjusting for Gender Differences

Enables Clear Dialogue with the Opposite Sex

MEN AND WOMEN TALKING

MEN AND WOMEN generally use different styles to communicate. If we don't understand these differences, we run the risk of miscommunication, frustration, disappointment, and resentment. By tuning in to these differences, we can experience more impactful exchanges and maintain deeper, more meaningful and successful relationships at work and in all aspects of our lives.

In this chapter we examine these gender-based communication styles, including the differences in how men and women tend to:

* Assimilate information

* Interpret conversations

* Approach problem solving

* Demonstrate leadership skills

* Argue perspectives

* Deal with personal issues

No style is right or wrong, only different, and that is what can be challenging and interesting. If we understand the differences and adjust our communication style appropriately, we can have more success when communicating with the opposite sex.

I don't mean to suggest that all men and women communicate exactly in these styles. As with any other generalization, there are countless exceptions, and each of us is a unique individual. Research does tell us, however, that most of us do have at least some of these gender-based tendencies.

MEN AND WOMEN WORKING TOGETHER

Because we're working and communicating with each other every day, knowing the differences in gender communication is vital. Much has already been written about personality, values, and behavioural differences in communication. Now it's time to bring gender differences into the equation.

If you're a manager or other leader, insight into gender-based communication differences equips you to tailor your message to the specific needs of the men and women on your team, helping them reach their potential and maintain high levels of performance. A happy, respectful workplace is productive, efficient, and creative, with little down time and almost no turnover—all good for the bottom line!

Managers who know about brain differences can look at management and supervision, meetings and alliances, work life and even home life differently. For example, a savvy manager will know that women focus on building consensus. And because of how they process information, they're often trying to reduce heated arguments. This doesn't mean a woman doesn't like a good argument; however, if it gets hostile and she gets stressed, her body will start producing the "bonding" hormone oxytocin, which will prompt her to take steps to calm the situation down. An astute manager will notice how women are trying to help an interaction with their oxytocin- and word-based relational approach.

Because women have so much white brain matter, they may take longer to answer a question because they're filtering it through the article they read this morning or what their boss said two days ago. Think of it like sorting in a computer. They're doing a huge sort through the entire database to arrive at an answer.

The savvy manager will also understand that men are typically more aggressive in their communications, more argumentative about their ideas, and more vocal about their opinions. They will know to watch carefully for the male look of "eyes glazing over" in response to people who use a lot of words.

Women, think about this

Let's say you call your business associate to remind him about an upcoming meeting with an important client, giving him a change in date, place, and time as well as the reason for the change. You now feel you have fulfilled your responsibility and you assume he will adjust his calendar.

But, did you check to see that this was a good time for him to talk? Perhaps he was working on an important document and did not focus on your call or the information you gave him. In fact, when the appointment arrives, he may well fail to show up, claiming you had not told him about it.

If this happens, you'll be understandably upset and disappointed, and honestly, so will he. However, guess what? You are certainly to blame as well for not checking to make sure he had in fact computed the message as intended and acted as you expected. A better approach would be to email an appointment change to his calendar or text the change to his phone—or at least ask him if this is a good time to talk and make sure he has understood what you need him to do.

Men, think about this

If your female colleague is telling you about her recent meeting with a prospective new client, she will appreciate you listening carefully to all that transpired without interrupting her with comments or questions until she has offered as many details as she wishes to share. In other words, practice Active Listening and do not offer input until she is done. She will greatly appreciate your listening skills and welcome any suggestions you might offer when her "story" is completed.

HOW ARE MEN AND WOMEN'S BRAINS DIFFERENT?

The female brain

The female brain tends to have 15 to 20 percent more blood flow at any given moment than men's brains, meaning more activity. In fact, women's brains are more active at rest than are men's brains when engaged.

Women's brains have 40 percent more connections between the emotional and thought-processing areas, causing women to experience emotions more readily and communicate them more fully.

The memory centre is larger in women's brains than in men's. Women typically retain more complex information.

Language tends to occur in both the left and right hemisphere of a woman's brain, as compared to much more predominantly in the left hemisphere in a man's brain. When reading, writing, and speaking are all factored in, women generally use more words than men in a day, but only marginally, as men catch up when gathered in mixed company. Women's brains have more active sensorial and emotive centres, with better linkage to language centres.

Women's greater neural emphasis is on oxytocin, a bonding chemical (as compared to the male chemical of competition and aggression, testosterone). Quite often in conversation, a man will try to compete while a woman tries to bond.

The male brain

Men's cerebellums tends to be larger than women's. The cerebellum is an action and physical movement centre. This means men tend to communicate more nonverbally, with more emphasis on movement and physicality, while women make greater use of words.

Men's senses don't generally work as well as women's; men don't process as much emotion; and they

don't tend to link as much complex emotion or sensorial detail to words.

Men's brains enter a rest or
"zone-out" state more easily
than women's—many times
per day in fact, compared to
only during sleep for women.
Men's brains also enter a rest
state when quantities of words become overwhelming
during communication.

> Men's brains circulate more
> testosterone than women's.
> Testosterone is a competition/
> aggression chemical.

Men's brains circulate more testosterone than wom-
en's. Testosterone is a competition/aggression chemical.

With fewer connections between the rational,
thought-processing side of the brain and the sensing,
communicative side, many men really do not like to
talk about feelings. They are more interested in concrete black-and-white issues. They prefer to do one
thing at a time and focus on it fully, and have little
patience or understanding for how women seem to flit
from one topic to another.

DIFFERENCES IN VERBAL COMMUNICATION

If you're a woman, you may sometimes wonder how your male colleagues can get into a heated discussion during a business meeting, end the meeting with issues unresolved, yet walk out of the room as if they're the best of friends.

And if you're a man, you may get frustrated when talking with your female co-workers about one topic and they bring fourteen more topics into the conversation—all of which seem totally unrelated.

We all know that men and women think and act differently, both at work and at home, but knowing there are differences between people is only half the battle. To have successful working relationships with members of the opposite sex, you also have to know why those differences matter and what to do about them. The good news is that, with a little insight, you can overcome the apparent communication and behavioural challenges that can plague any workplace and gain greater understanding of each other.

If you think about verbal communication for a moment, you might immediately have some "Ahas" about your communication with the other gender. A powerful illustration might take place in a meeting of your managerial team. If, for instance, a woman leads the meeting, there may be more discussion, more words used, more interest in emotive, sensorial, and relational detail—in short, more about process. If a man leads the meeting, it may be shorter and not as immersed in relational details—more oriented to the bottom line and direct results.

If a conflict should emerge in the meeting, the men may become louder and more competitive as their chosen method of resolving the conflict. Their testosterone level increases with the increase of stress hormones.

> Women's brains have more active sensorial and emotive centres, with better linkage to language centres.

The women, on the other hand, may become quieter and try to find ways to restore equilibrium and keep relationships intact, rather than becoming edgy with competition. Women's oxytocin levels increase with the increase in their stress hormones. This brings out the "nurturing" side, concerning them with how others are feeling.

Some women, of course, are quite competitive and loud, and some men are soft-spoken and non-competitive. The fact that exceptions exist does actually help prove the rule!

Differences in speaking

To have more impactful conversations across the genders, we need to adjust our communication style to suit who we are speaking with. It's helpful to keep these general points in mind about how men and women tend to speak:

Men

- ★ Use short phrases (like bullet points)
- ★ Omit details
- ★ Want the "bottom line" as quickly as possible
- ★ Prefer to problem solve (fix it!)
- ★ Have a "product" fixation (just get there!)
- ★ Tend to be more single minded, less inclusive when working toward a goal

Women

- ★ Speak in paragraphs
- ★ Give the narrative account of situations
- ★ Include all the descriptions
- ★ Have a "process" fixation (how do we get there?)
- ★ "Bottom line" comes in later
- ★ Tend to be more creative and innovative in problem solving
- ★ Tend to seek more involvement when working toward a goal (prefer a collaborative approach and tend to give credit where credit is due)

We assimilate information differently

Women

- ★ Store memory in more parts of their brains
- ★ Notice many details and make instantaneous connections to things from the past
- ★ Are better able to see patterns

Men

- ★ Tend to see a situation in isolation
- ★ Keep conversations "to the point at hand"

★ Focus quickly on the important features of one isolated problem

We solve problems differently

Women

★ Tend to explore all possible solutions before settling on one
★ Apply multi-thinking to problem solving

Men

★ Tend to attack problems by isolating them
★ Consider action the imperative

We work differently in teams

Women

★ Feel rewarded through working together on teams

Men

★ Feel rewarded by beating the competition and winning the game

"What Do You Think?" Means

She

★ This is an opening to a conversation or exploration of thoughts and feelings

He

★ I am being asked for closure: to give an opinion or make a decision

Expressing an idea at a meeting

She

★ Makes a suggestion and asks for input of others

He

★ Clearly states the idea or action to be taken

A colleague is experiencing a personal problem, so

She

★ Asks for details and discusses the problem to show her concern and support

He

- ★ Focuses on solving the issue or avoids the subject to demonstrate respect for his colleague's independence and privacy

Arguments are best supported by

She

- ★ Personal experiences and the experiences of others

He

- ★ Facts, surveys, careful logic

Success means

She

- ★ Being valued while accomplishing common goals

He

- ★ Winning

In summary

What Women Want

* ★ Understanding before action

What Men Want

* ★ Action

ONCE UPON A TIME . . .
BRAIN EVOLUTION

To understand these gender differences in communication styles, it helps to look back into human evolution. Once upon a time about a million years ago, communities consisted of hunters (men) and gatherers (women). The hunters left every morning and tried to hunt food for the community. The gatherers stayed closer to home base and gathered the nuts and berries and made preparations for the food the men would bring back. So, as far back as scientists can tell, women and men had different roles, and as a result, their brains developed in different ways.

For example, we've already noted that a man's brain goes in and out of a rest state all day. When our male ancestors sat in hiding while waiting for their prey, they had to be quiet and disengaged. They didn't want to scare away their potential dinner. So their brain evolved to learn to engage, disengage, engage, and disengage throughout the day.

Women, on the other hand, couldn't do that. They had to be on high alert all day, protecting themselves and their children as they gathered necessities and tended to the community's needs. Their brains evolved to be always active.

In fact, if you look at functional MRIs of a man's and woman's brain at rest, you'll see that the woman's brain is busy and firing everywhere, whereas the man's brain is quiet. This is not to say that one gender is better than the other; it's simply an illustration of one of the many differences between men and women and how it evolved.

BRAIN WIRING

So, what else is different from a brain-wiring perspective? Here are a few highlights:

* **Brain chemicals**—Men produce more testosterone and women produce more oxytocin. Testosterone increases aggression, while oxytocin increases the "tend-and-befriend" impulse. These chemicals are significant drivers in a person's brain.

* **Cycles**—While women have a 28-day cycle, men have a cycle every day. Their testosterone spikes in the morning when they wake up (so they can go out and hunt) and wanes through the afternoon and evening, rising again early the next morning.

* **Brain matter**—Men have more grey matter, while women have more white matter. The grey matter is used for local processing of thoughts and tasks. The white matter is what connects everything. This is why when a woman is processing an emotional event, she will do so immediately. All the interconnections make processing faster in her mind. A man is processing locally and will

do so for a longer time. He doesn't have the same connections to draw from.

★ **Hierarchy**—While both men and women understand hierarchy, men really understand it. Whoever brought back the biggest animal from the hunt received the most status in the community. So that desire to be "top dog" and get their point across is innate in men. Likewise, women wanted the security of being with the men who could provide the

> Managers who know about brain differences can look at management and supervision, meetings and alliances, work life and even home life differently.

most food for the family, which is why even today women (no matter what their income level or social status) want to be associated with successful men. It's hardwired.

Of course, there are exceptions to every rule. The spectrum of male and female brains contains infinite gradations. There are also "bridge brains," situated in the middle of the spectrum, with characteristics of both the male and female brains.

TIPS FOR BETTER COMMUNICATION

The following points can help you ease daily workplace communication challenges.

For men speaking to women

★ Keep women's white matter in mind. They are not jumping from topic to topic to annoy you. In their brain, everything is connected.

★ Remember that women "tend and befriend." As a result, they have a tendency to use up-talk (ending a sentence with the voice going higher, like when asking a question). Or they say such things as "What do you think?" This does not mean they don't know what to think. They simply want to gain consensus.

★ Understand that women all over the world tend to use more emotionally loaded words when they communicate. So they use high-drama phrases and words such as "always" and "never" much more often than men do.

★ Give more details. Women like them.

★ Make eye contact, it shows you are paying attention.

★ Validate feelings by using Active Listening (repeating back) to show you have heard the intended message.

★ Don't fix, listen. Try not to interrupt.

★ Save your competitiveness for people who seem game to relate in that way.

★ Ask questions, and pay attention to body language.

★ Spend time in process.

★ Keep your guy friends!

For women speaking to men

★ If you want to talk to a man about something critical and you think he's going to be defensive, make sure he is not focused on other matters. So, for example, avoid speaking to him in the midst of the 9 a.m. meeting or after hours at the company dinner. The key, as always, is communication: ask to make sure the time and place are right for him.

★ Don't jump from subject to subject, and do condense your thoughts into short sentences. Men have a word limit (this has been scientifically tested), and once they reach their limit, they can't process more information.

★ Remember that a man's brain shifts into rest state throughout the day. So when you're talking to him and he's fidgeting, tapping his fingers on the table, or even doodling during the meeting, it doesn't necessarily mean he's bored or not interested. In fact, it probably means just the opposite. He's unconsciously forcing himself to stay alert, keeping his brain active with that movement.

★ Give the bottom line first.

★ Ask if he wants more details.

★ Speak in short phrases.

★ Be direct, no "hint" language (they do not "get it").

* Keep the pitch of your voice low, but speak loudly enough to be heard.

* Check with him to see if he can receive your message (Is this a good time? When would be a good time?). He may be in a resting stage and not able to take it in.

* Keep your girl friends!

CLOSING THE GREAT DIVIDE

The key now is to apply this information. Stay conscious and aware of the differences between the sexes. By adjusting what you say and how you say it to fit different gender styles, you can ease the frustrations in work-related communications and build professional relationships based on understanding, collaboration, rapport, and trust.

GENDER DIFFERENCES EXERCISE

Guys: If your female colleague comes to you to discuss a project you are working on together and you are in the middle of something you need to finish, be honest and tell her it is not a good time to talk. Then offer a better time, rather than half listening to her and not getting the details you actually need to solve the problem. She will appreciate your candid explanation. Then, when you do have the conversation, try to focus on her concerns.

Ladies: When you need to speak with a male colleague, be sure to check that the timing is good for him. If he is focused on another piece of work, he may not process your conversation completely, resulting in miscommunication. Then, neither of you will get the desired outcome. You might want to confirm the time designated for this discussion via a short email (with a very direct subject line) or a brief text (use whatever technology he uses the most).

KEY TAKEAWAY POINTS FOR
SECRET #4: GENDER DIFFERENCES

1. In general, men and women have evolved to think and communicate differently. Knowing these differences helps you communicate more effectively.

2. Ladies, be less anecdotal when explaining something to your male colleagues, and watch your voice tone and pitch.

3. Fellows, be more patient, offer more details and maintain eye contact during exchanges with your female colleagues. Also, appreciate that even if you have stretched to have a conversation about "feelings" and think it is done, she may not be finished.

4. Appreciate the differences but do not let them confound you. Turn to your same-sex colleagues for understanding and support, while also learning to adjust your style for the opposite sex.

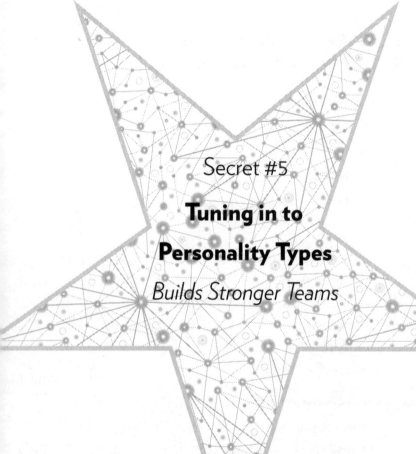

Secret #5

Tuning in to Personality Types

Builds Stronger Teams

EMPOWERMENT THROUGH PERSONALITY TYPES

A T WORK, you may be either part of a team, or a team leader. How can you help your team achieve high performance, productivity, efficiency, and creativity? One important factor is personality type. The better the team leader understands the people on their team, the more likely they'll be able to empower team members toward autonomy, mastery, and purpose.

And the better team members know each other's types, the more easily they can leverage their gifts and find ways to get around their drawbacks.

By understanding each other's personality type, we can better appreciate why some people need more time and information to make decisions while others need more direction and support. We can appreciate the "ideas people" and admire the organizers and the competent results-oriented doers. Leaders and team members can better appreciate and understand each other, and the team can function at a high level, helping everyone reach their potential.

FOUR PERSONALITY TYPES

Determining what personality type our team members are can free them to do their best work using their most natural skills and talents. Personality typing helps leaders put together effective teams with exactly the right mix of complementary skill sets and traits.

There are many different typing systems. I use a system that works with these four types:

- ★ Supporters
- ★ Analyzers
- ★ Controllers
- ★ Promoters

I like that this system uses descriptive type names, rather than colours or initials, as in some other systems. These names give us an immediate sense of the personality type.

> Determining what personality type our team members are can free them to do their best work using their most natural skills and talents.

Keep in mind that each personality type has their gifts and drawbacks as well as particular styles of dealing with responsibilities and challenges. The key is to understand and appreciate the strengths and weaknesses of each type. By learning how to leverage the positive attributes of each team member, we help the team achieve a win/win for everyone. Communicating effectively with each team member is how we realize our common aims in a timely and effective manner.

So let's get started with examining the basic traits of these four personality types so we can adjust our communication styles to suit them.

Supporters

Key words

- ★ Amiable
- ★ Caring
- ★ Understanding
- ★ Attentive listeners
- ★ Sensitive
- ★ Gentle
- ★ Approachable
- ★ Easy-going
- ★ Emotionally honest

Gifts: Supporters allow others a safe, loving environment to be who they are.

Benefits of the Supporting style

People with a supporting style are perceived by others as casual and likeable. Though responsive to people, they generally let others take the initiative in social situations. Supporters try to minimize interpersonal conflict, and they find it difficult to turn down a request, because they want to be helpful, even if they must subordinate personal interests. Their understanding and friendly approach to people is non-threatening and makes them easy to be with. Supporters are often very intuitive.

Not usually highly competitive people, Supporters don't impose themselves on others or try to convince others of their point of view. They tend to be more concerned with feelings and relationships than with logic or tasks. Unpretentious people, they tend to be permissive with others.

Supporters usually seek close, warm, and lasting relationships. They are good listeners who take time with people to help them feel at ease. They approach others on the basis of relationship rather than task and are accepting of many personality types, partly because of their need to be liked. Supporters will do all they can to complete the tasks they commit to, as they are service oriented.

Perceived drawbacks

On the one hand, the supporter may be perceived as easy-going, affable, gentle, eager to please, and pleasant. On the other hand they may also be seen as wishy-washy, unwilling to take a stand, overly yielding, and unmotivated.

They avoid hurt feelings at all costs and may often feel resentment as a result. Responsive to praise, they may be too eager to please, pretending to consent to and agree with people even when they disagree and don't intend to consent.

A person such as this may lack interest in planning and goal-setting and may need structure and specific descriptions of the task to be completed. There are times when more direct and honest feedback to others would benefit them. They may need to learn to stand up for their ideas and be willing to risk the disapproval of others.

They may be more effective as they apply relationship skills to the task at hand.

Because of the supporter's dislike of conflict, they may tend to withhold unpleasant information.

On the job

In a job setting, supporters will generally be cooperative and willing to be of service to others or to the company. They will tend to work through the structure in order to prevent interpersonal misunderstandings and, therefore, will accept supervision readily. They try to please others by doing what is expected of them. They like reassurance that what they are doing is acceptable and respond to the personal attention they get from superiors. Once having formed an emotional allegiance, they will be loyal workers. They welcome direction from others. If they believe their ideas can benefit others, they will put them forth in a non-threatening manner.

Analyzers

Key words

- ★ Thinker
- ★ Problem solver
- ★ Wise
- ★ Committed
- ★ Loyal
- ★ Efficient
- ★ Accepting
- ★ Dedicated

Gifts: Analyzers contribute order, justice, wisdom, and excellence to the world.

Benefits of the Analyzing style

Analyzers tend to take a problem solving approach to situations. Oriented more toward ideas and concepts than relationships or feelings, they prefer study and contemplation to immediate action and give a thoughtful, even hesitant, impression. As a result of their restrained and unassuming way, they tend to be a steadying influence in a group.

Because they are deliberate and unaggressive, they usually wait for others to come to them rather than offering an opinion. Though they tend not to initiate relationships, others will seek them out for their patience and good listening skills. Having once formed an emotional bond, they are loyal.

Analyzers typically collect a great many facts and opinions before making a decision. They like to take a slow, measured approach when dealing with any situation or when researching data. Serious and precise, they consult with others as one of the ways to gather information. They hate to be wrong and will avoid it at all costs, so they usually wait until they are sure of their ground before they offer opinions. In addition, they tend not to seek personal recognition, preferring to work in the background in a problem solving role.

Others perceive them as academic and as taking themselves very seriously.

Though they appear unemotional, they can be tough and arbitrary when needed.

They prefer to avoid interpersonal confrontation and conflict.

Perceived drawbacks

While Analyzers may be perceived as knowledgeable, expert, steady, dependable, and unflappable, they may also be seen as boring, tedious, withheld, uncommunicative, and incapable of making a decision.

Analyzers are great ones for "buyer's remorse," because they continue to gather pertinent data even after a decision has been made. In relationships, they do not easily risk or trust. Personal disclosure comes with great difficulty, as their emotions are deep set.

They may become tense or immobilized when confronted with chaos and ambiguity.

On the job

On the job, Analyzers generally take an orderly, systematic approach to the task at hand. Detailed and thorough, they usually like things to be rational and well organized. They work at tasks persistently, conscientiously, and industriously, without pause.

They work best in an environment with well-established rules and procedures, where their methodical efforts will be most effective. Not likely to thrive on hard competition, they fit more naturally in an advisory role. Their steady and quiet manner will often cause others to look to them for counsel, for the facts, and for precision.

Controllers

Key words

- ★ Driver
- ★ Independent

- ★ Decisive
- ★ Competent
- ★ Clear
- ★ Responsible
- ★ Ambitious
- ★ Self-confident
- ★ Leads by example

Gifts: Controllers offer inspiration, guidance, and leadership to the world.

Benefits of the Controlling style

Controllers tend to be active, independent, and ambitious, giving an appearance of self-confidence. They take the initiative with others individually and in groups and enjoy orchestrating things with a take-charge attitude. They are generally strong-willed and forceful and are willing to confront others about their ideas and attitudes. They usually make decisions easily and rapidly, which conveys a sense of efficiency and perhaps urgency. Generally, Controllers are punctual and keep their agreements as if they were sacred vows.

They also tend to do things in a fast-paced manner and have little patience for a slower-paced approach to accomplishing tasks.

Controllers like information and often make it their business to discern the who, what, where, and how of any given situation. Preferring order and organization, Controllers can make order from chaos easily and naturally. Because they are likely to want to get the job done first before taking time to work on interpersonal relationships, they may experience the "lonely-at-the-top" syndrome.

Perceived drawbacks

While the Controller may be seen as efficient, cool, competent, organized, and in-the-know, they may also be perceived as arrogant, power driven, self-centred, rigid, and impatient. As a result of their strong task-oriented approach, Controllers may not demonstrate much emotion.

Controllers like to be fully in charge of any situation and may resent others having power over them; they want to run all parts of their own life. They can be demanding at times and may work to meet self-described objectives without realizing that their behaviour might be irritating to others. They will be seen as competent and determined, but at times may push too hard and be too critical of others. They will look to other people for results but may not offer them encouragement, inspiration, or support.

People with a Controlling style tend to lack patience and may not find it rewarding to work with the same project over a long period of time. They may need to strengthen their ability to listen to others and recognize the importance of feelings as well as logic.

> Controllers take the initiative with others individually and in groups and enjoy orchestrating things with a take-charge attitude.

The need for personal success may limit their ability to cooperate with others in accomplishing organizational goals. Not having the situation under their control may raise their anxiety level.

On the job

On the job, Controllers generally respond to a fast-moving challenge and get bored if they find the pace too slow. They tend to set objectives and work toward them in an orderly fashion. Because they direct energy toward task results, others will naturally accept their authority and leadership.

Promoters

Key words

- ★ Expressive
- ★ Positive attitude
- ★ Creative
- ★ Energetic
- ★ Friendly
- ★ Active
- ★ Relaxed
- ★ Fun-loving
- ★ Leader

Gifts: Promoters express and allow enthusiasm and aliveness in others.

Benefits of the Promoting style

Promoters tend to get involved with people in active, rapidly moving situations. They generally like exciting activities of an inspirational nature. They are usually stimulating to be with, socially outgoing, friendly, lively, and personable.

Promoters like to have fun and will seek people who like to play and be spontaneous. They are aware of and concerned with the feelings and ideas of others, and try to include them in their plans, especially recreational.

Promoters are often sports minded and tend to be highly competitive. Because of a somewhat dramatic and emotional nature, they may think out loud and convince others of their position, when they themselves have already moved on to other ideas.

For Promoters in managerial positions, an organized, methodical support team often keeps their sometimes erratic ways and lack of detail-mindedness in check.

Perceived drawbacks

While Promoters may be seen as exciting, provocative, fun-loving, personable, and energetic, they may also be seen as emotional, disorganized, loud or aggressive, erratic, and approval seeking.

People with a Promoting style usually lack concern for details and may move forward too rapidly before completing a task. They may jump to conclusions based on intuition or a hunch, without sufficient factual information. They will sometimes settle for less than the best to get things done.

Even though they are viewed as socially outgoing and forceful, others may perceive Promoters as manipulative or conniving. Their enthusiasm may come across as instability or egoism. They can be given to exaggeration.

On the job

On the job, promoters are often eager to please others, especially those who respond to their outgoing ways. They are usually open with their feelings and try to be helpful in interpersonal situations. Promoters are usually popular with co-workers and their imagination and enthusiasm act as a motivating force.

Motivated by inspirational leadership, Promoters may try to achieve status and prestige by attaching themselves to people they believe have the qualities of leadership or charisma. They want recognition from both peers and superiors.

They work best in a setting that provides some structure to support them with the planning and follow-through that is unnatural to them.

Communicating effectively with each team member is how we realize our common aims in a timely and effective manner.

SUCCESS FORMULA USING PERSONALITY TYPES

As you get a feel for the four basic personality types, you'll become able to leverage the particular strengths and gifts of each employee or team member, and mitigate their weaknesses. The magic of personality types in the workplace is that, once you understand them, you can combine them to build an effective high-performance team.

Below is a quick equation to help you visualize how these types can be combined. At a glance, you can see how our differences are key to a dynamic and balanced workplace.

Controller   Results & Accomplishments

Plus

Supporter   Relationships & Stability

Plus

Analyzer   Precision & Accuracy

Plus

Promoter   Involvement & Enthusiasm

Equals

Team Effectiveness   Balance & Partnership

SPEAKING THEIR LANGUAGE THROUGH "STYLE FLEXING"

Once you understand the personality style of a co-
worker, you're much more likely to communicate effectively with them. If you're a fellow team member, you'll
have important insight into how to work with them in
a spirit of true collaboration. If you're in a leadership

position, you'll know how to draw on their strengths and support them in any weaknesses.

Once you know an individual's personality type, you can modify your presentation to match it. This is called "style flexing" or "speaking their language." Essentially, there are two ways to modify your messages to match another person's personality type.

> If we understand and appreciate who our team members are, we can then flex the appropriate communication style to leverage their outstanding traits to the advantage of the entire team.

1. **Modify what you say**—that is, what methods, words, and phrases you use. Certain words have more meaning to some styles than others. As you'll see below, you can choose what you say according to what ideas and language have the most impact on and meaning for each personality style.

2. **Modify how you say it**—fast, slow, detailed, conceptual, emotional, etc.

SIGNIFICANT PHRASES FOR STYLE FLEXING

PROMOTER	SUPPORTER
"We have a unique approach for you to consider."	"Everyone is going to like the way it cuts down on overtime."
"This idea is going to pay off even more in the years ahead."	"Your friend Bill Smith over at xyz company is also taking this approach."
"This idea ties in very well with the principle of . . . "	"The plan we have here has traditionally worked for us in the past. If you talk to those who have used it, you will find it has been most effective."
ANALYZER	CONTROLLER
"I've got the entire play spelled out here, step by step."	"I only need five minutes of your time."
"There are several alternative ways to tackle your problem."	"We can start on it tomorrow!"
"Why don't you take our program and study it for a few days?"	"I am going to skip the details and just hit the highlights."

If we understand and appreciate who our team members are, we can then flex the appropriate communication style to leverage their outstanding traits to the advantage of the entire team. We can also help them to recognize and minimize their less stellar tendencies. This will result in less miscommunication, frustration, disappointment, and resentment. The outcome will be a higher happiness factor in a more respectful workplace.

With this very positive environment we will have the means for higher performance, increased productivity, efficiency, and creativity. The final result will be a better bottom line due to less down time, little turnover and greater team engagement. In all, a much more achievement-oriented architecture for your organization!

PERSONALITY TYPING EXERCISE

Choose a colleague and try to determine which personality type they are. Then, decide what message format would suit their style.

★ Are they results-oriented, impatient, confident, competent, and organized?

★ Do they have lots of ideas but have trouble focusing on one and completing it?

★ Do they need lots of time to make a decision, but generally do create good systems and analyze situations well given enough data?

★ Do they require lots of direction, reassurance, and support?

Once you have determined their personality type, review the description of that type and make a short list of key points. Think about how to best communicate with this person in future interactions. What are their strengths and weaknesses? Are there ways you could adjust your communication with them to help them focus their work, accomplish better results, and achieve greater personal satisfaction?

KEY TAKEAWAY POINTS FROM SECRET #5: PERSONALITY TYPES

1. Each of the four personality types has strengths and weaknesses.

2. Knowledge of these qualities equips you to build successful, productive, high-performance teams and facilitate greater satisfaction for each team member.

3. Each personality type has a preferred style of communicating. Understanding this can enhance your ability to "style flex," or modify your communication to suit each person. This results in less confusion, miscommunication, and resentment and greater efficiency, creativity, and all-round happiness at work.

Communication

Summary

I TRUST THAT YOU have gained new insights into the complexities of communication in the workplace. You now have effective strategies, such as Active Listening, for dealing with difficult situations. You have learned why and how to shift from victim to victor through accountability and assertiveness. And with your new understanding of different gender and personality styles, you're equipped to empower yourself and others on your team.

Remember, though: knowledge alone isn't enough. To become good at anything, you must practice. To become a more effective communicator, I encourage you to use these skills at every opportunity. In time, you'll find you establish a new communication style that embodies the principles in this book. As with any other skill, the more you use these strategies, the more likely they will become your default approach to communicating at work—and in all your relationships!

> Knowledge alone isn't enough. To become good at anything, you must practice.

Whether your goal is a stronger team and higher productivity at work, or reduced stress and greater health for yourself, becoming a clear and proactive communicator will help.

Remember, the only thing you truly have control over is your ATTITUDE, so keep yours positive . . . for a more efficient workplace and a happier life!

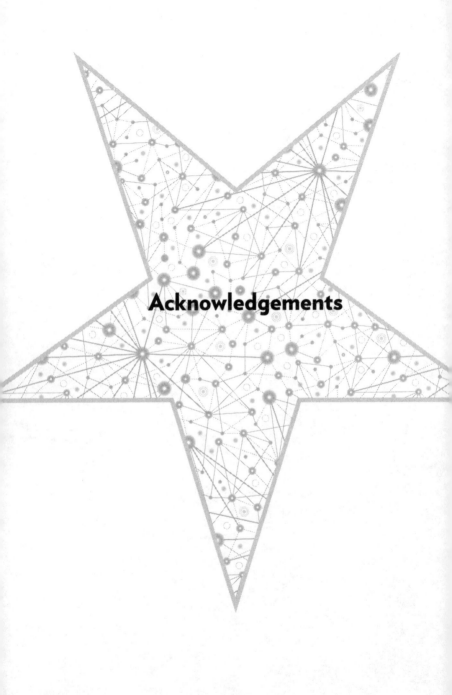

Acknowledgements

ONE DAY IN 2002, my son, Marc, said to me, "Mom, you're really good at this, why don't you do it for real?" And I said, "I do do this for real!"

He said, "No, do it for money!"

I said, "Don't be ridiculous, I am old and I am a dental hygienist." He rolled his eyes and told me to go and get a business card. So I did.

Thank you, Marc!

Eventually, when it became apparent that I really had something to say about communication, many people encouraged me to write a book. At first, this seemed like a daunting task. I thought about it for a very long time before starting, but I'm glad I persisted.

I began with blogging to get my ideas down in writing. When I did finally commit to creating the manuscript, I must admit that the initial draft came rather quickly. Without the tireless, supportive direction of book designer Jan Westendorp and editor Marial Shea, I certainly could not have completed this project.

I owe a great debt to my son, Marc, not only for sending me out into the world with business cards in hand. He also offered the first round of proofreading on this book, and was very good at it. My daughter, Ali, was helpful too, offering her experience from the books she has written. Finally, my husband, Yale, has always encouraged me to write a book, as he feels I express myself well. Thanks to all of you!

ABOUT THE AUTHOR

Sandy Chernoff, RDH, B.Sc., is the owner of Soft Skills for Success, a consulting firm that provides customized, interactive workshops and coaching sessions in a wide variety of skills, including:

★ Communication
★ Time management and goal setting
★ Leadership
★ Transition and change management
★ Team building
★ Stress deflection

Since 1995, Sandy has worked with corporate and non-profit organizations and individuals across North

America. In her popular presentations, she engages audiences with her energetic, humorous, and interactive style in an atmosphere conducive to retentive learning.

Sandy lives in Vancouver, BC, with her husband. They have two adult children, a daughter-in-law, and two grandsons. Travelling, keeping fit, enjoying healthy eating, doing volunteer work, and spending time with family and friends keep her busy when she is not presenting sessions.

To learn more about Sandy's work, or to subscribe to her blog or contact her directly, please visit her website: www.softskillsforsuccess.com.